Cat Got Your Tongue?

Powerful Public Speaking Skills
& Presentation Strategies
for Confident Communication or,
How to Create the Purrfect Speech

DIANE WINDINGLAND

ISBN-10: 0-983-00786-1
ISBN-13: 978-0-9830078-6-9

Contents

Preface

Don't let the cat get YOUR tongue!

In this book you will discover how to:

- MANAGE the fear of public speaking
- Melt the "plastic person" and become AUTHENTIC
- Learn how to PRACTICE your speech without having to memorize it all
- Transform your IDEAS into speeches quickly
- Discover powerful speech STRUCTURES
- Learn time-tested RHETORICAL DEVICES to create memorable phrases
- "Find the Funny" and effectively use HUMOR
- Develop DYNAMIC Openings and closings
- Create engaging STORIES that will keep an audience hanging on your every word
- Learn key DELIVERY techniques

Acknowledgements

I thank all Toastmasters, past and present, who have contributed to the communication and leadership development of millions around the world, myself included.

I thank my husband, Kim Windingland, who not only offers encouragement, but also allows me to regularly evaluate his speeches.

A special thanks to the following people who made specific comments or recommendations for this book:

Paul Berghout
Chuck Christian
Nadia Giordana
Daniel Nelson
Lindagail Roy
Joe Sharp
Tamara Weber

Finally, a shout-out to one of my biggest encouragers, Vitalia Bryn-Pundyk, owner of SpeakerBiz, The School for Speaker Success. It was through her encouragement that I decided to explore becoming a professional speaker.

Introduction

What difference could you make if instead of being controlled by the fear of public speaking you could manage that fear and have your voice heard?

What difference could you make if you spoke with power, persuasion and a more polished presence?

What a difference you could make!

Great speeches have made a difference throughout history. A few examples from American history:

Abraham Lincoln's Gettysburg Address called for a "new birth of freedom" which would promote unity and equality.

John F. Kennedy's Inauguration Address called people to a collective altruism. "And so my fellow Americans: ask not what your country can do for you—ask what you can do for your country."

Martin Luther King's "I Have a Dream" speech called for racial equality and an end to discrimination.

These men made a difference. Their speeches made a difference. Your speeches can make a difference, too.

But, has the "cat got your tongue?"

Theories abound as to the origin of the idiom, "Cat got your tongue?" Which essentially is asking "Why aren't you talking?" One theory is that the saying stems from an ancient Middle East custom of punishing a liar by ripping out his tongue and feeding it to the king's cats. Another theory is that the saying comes from the time of English sailing ships, when fear of a whipping with a cat-o'-nine tails or "cat" could silence a sailor. More recent explanations claim a nineteenth century origin of when a parent or other adult would try to get an unusually quiet child to talk. Of course, now with all the texting that teens do, the phrase could be changed to "Cat got your thumbs?"

Whatever the origin of "Cat got your tongue?" when it comes to giving a presentation, at work, at school, in your community or at important life events, silence or reluctance to speak can at best be uncomfortable and at worst keep you from achieving your full potential and making the difference in the world that you were meant to make.

This book will address the fear of public speaking and then quickly move into practical techniques that you can use right away to make a difference in your world by making a difference in your presentations.

You can read the book from start to finish, or jump to a section that addresses a specific need.

How to Manage the Fear of Public Speaking

I am not going to tell you how to overcome the fear of public speaking. Instead, I am going to offer suggestions on how to manage the fear so that it is not debilitating. If you try too hard to suppress the symptoms of speaking anxiety—the shaky hands, the red face, the stiff or jerky body movements, the dry mouth, the trembling voice—you can end up in a vicious cycle that only worsens your anxiety and increases the expression of nervous symptoms. It can lead to an overwhelming sense of dread that can hinder you personally and professionally. Break out of the vicious cycle, find your voice and speak with increasing confidence.

First, realize that you are not alone. The fear of public speaking is famously widespread. And it can occur at all levels of speaking, from beginner to professional. Recently, I sat in the front row during a well-paid professional speaker's presentation and noticed that his hands shook as he spoke. Nobody really seemed to care.

Second, realize that there are actions that you can take to manage the fear. Action is the antidote to fear. If you want to play the game, you have to act. There is both an inner game and an outer game in a winning presentation. Did you catch on to the sports metaphor? If you are sports-minded, you can apply many of the same performance techniques to giving a speech. You might even consider "cross training" your fear by becoming involved in a sport (or a creative endeavor) that has a performance component.

For several years, in my forties, I was involved in karate. As part of the class we occasionally had to practice our forms "tournament style" in which we simulated tournament competition. We would introduce ourselves to the group and perform our forms individually. At first I dreaded it. My heart would race and my breathing would quicken just before it was my turn. And then, I would hold my breath during the form. My face would turn as red as a baboon's bottom! I was afraid of making a mistake and looking stupid. I knew that even my best performance was a far cry from perfection. Over time it became easier. After a few months, I was hardly nervous at all when we did "tournament style." Part of the reason was repetition—of being regularly exposed to that which caused fear. The other part was the inner and outer games I played with myself to manage that fear. Many of the same techniques can be applied to managing the fear of public speaking.

The most important action you can take to manage the fear of public speaking is the unseen mental preparation, the inner game.

The Inner Game

1. Know Your Audience

If you are not familiar with your audience, you will need to do a little research. For my professional speaking presentations, I will conduct 3-10 informational interviews with audience members, often from different functional areas. What do they value? What fears or challenges do they have? What experiences have shaped them? In the process of getting to know my audience, I would begin to almost fall in love with them. When you fall in love, your focus changes.

2. Mentally Focus on Giving the Audience a Gift

Changing my focus from me to them was what made the biggest difference for me in managing my fear. I began to see my presentation as a gift I was giving to the audience. I was giving them a gift that could help them change for the positive what they might think, feel or do. My fear started to turn to excitement. Like a mother who can't wait for her children to open their birthday gifts that she had carefully selected just for them, I couldn't wait for my audience to receive the gift of my presentation.

3. Know Your Material
This is standard advice and still very important! You must know your material and I don't mean that you must memorize it. Don't memorize. Internalize. Be so familiar with your material that you can talk about it easily with friends. Also, know more than you would ever tell in a presentation. That way if you happen to forget something (and you will) you have extra material to access. Plus, remember that your audience doesn't know if you forgot something. As far as they know, the way you give a speech is how you intended to give it.

4. Accept the Fear
I call this radical acceptance. Don't condemn or berate yourself for having fear or having visible nervous symptoms. Allow it to just be. And allow yourself to be aware of the fear as you are speaking—it's there, but it doesn't have to paralyze you. You have the power to choose how to deal with it. Think about how

you would treat someone you love who has the same fear and treat yourself the same.

5. Give up Perfectionism.

Striving for perfection is healthy and admirable. Expecting achievement of perfection as the only acceptable outcome ensures that every performance will be a failure. The unreasonable and unrealistic expectation of perfection creates the kind of tension that causes people to "choke." To err is definitely human and in fact, our imperfections are what make us authentic and relatable.

6. Ask yourself—"What's the Worst That Can Happen?"

Sometimes fear can grow out of proportion to actual consequences. If you know what you are afraid of, ask yourself, "What's the worst that can happen?" And then, mentally plan how you will deal with it. Let's say you are afraid your hands are going to shake when you speak—what's the worst that can happen? People might think you are nervous? You might drop your notes? Whatever "the worst" is for you, address it. So what if people think you are nervous? Is that so bad? If you drop your notes, what will you do? Will you have them numbered so that they will be easy to reorder?

7. Visualize Success

What you focus on will be what you get. Think about what you want, not about what you don't want. I've noticed that in my son's soccer games that all too often when a player is trying to make a goal, he seems to kick the ball right at the goalie. He should kick where the goalie isn't, but instead focuses on the goalie. Similarly don't focus on all the negative that might happen, because you will be programming yourself negatively. Focus and visualize the optimum situation: an attentive audience and you as a confident speaker. Visualize how you will move and look as the speaker you want to be.

8. Meditate/Pray/Self-Hypnotize

The calming effects of meditation, prayer and self-hypnosis are well-documented. All three involve settling the mind and often result in a calming, deep breathing pattern which is the opposite of how you feel when you are afraid.

9. Consider outside help

If you still feel debilitating fear after trying some of the above techniques, you might want to enlist the help of a professional. There are mental health professionals and practitioners of other calming or behavioral modification techniques that can assist you in managing your fear.

Many people will say that you need to change your feelings and beliefs (the inner game) before you can change your actions (the outer game). However, I believe that feelings, beliefs and actions are interrelated. You can change one to affect the other. In public speaking, you can "fake it till you make it" to a certain extent. You can act as if you already are the speaker you wish to become.

The Outer Game

1. Structure Your Speech for Success
Don't make your speech too

complicated! Most people can only remember three main points, so try to have only three main points that you support with stories, examples and interesting facts.

2. Practice. Practice. Practice.

One of the biggest fears that people have about public speaking is that they are going to forget their speech, or that they will have poor delivery. Overlearning the material and practicing will help you gain confidence. Practice from keywords and allow yourself to say things differently from how you originally wrote the presentation. If you try to memorize a presentation and then, under stress, can't recall the exact phrase you memorized, your mind is more likely to draw a blank than if you simply practiced from concepts and key words. Practice your transitions between your key points as well, to help your delivery become smooth.   Memorizing the opening and closing can also help you feel more confident, and those are the parts that people are most likely to remember, anyway.

3. Vary Practice Conditions

Practicing under different conditions will help you deal with stress. One of my favorite places to practice is in the car while I'm driving. This divides my attention between the speech and driving (you probably DON'T want to practice in rush hour), which makes just giving the speech seem easier. If you have the opportunity to practice where you will be giving the presentation—take it!

4. Rehearse Live

There is nothing like a live rehearsal! Give your presentation or portions of it to your friends and family. Toastmaster clubs are a great place to practice and get feedback on presentations, too.

5. Reduce Risk: Have Checklists and Back Up Plans

Make a check list (notes, water, props, equipment, speaker introduction, etc.) and check it before you leave for your presentation. And, have a plan B. And a plan C. And a plan D. Almost anything that can go wrong eventually will. But some things are more likely to go wrong—technology for example. If you have a PowerPoint presentation, have a plan for what you will do if it doesn't work.

6. Have Coping Supports in Place

You know what your challenges are. What can help? Do you need some water for dry mouth? Room temperature water is probably best for your vocal cords. Do you need a small towel for sweaty palms? If your hands shake maybe small note cards are better than sheets of paper for your speaking notes. Do you tend to pace or rock? Try planting your feet in a comfortable stance and just staying in one spot unless you have a reason to move (e.g., making a point or talking to the other side of the audience on a large stage).

7. Warm Up

If I am driving to a speaking engagement alone, I almost always warm up my vocal cords by singing in the car, either to the radio or, more often to the "Do-Re-Mi" song. I also will slide my voice up and down, humming from low to high pitch and back again. I do this to improve the quality and range of my voice. You can also release some nervous tension by stretching your arms, neck and jaw, rolling your shoulders and clenching and unclenching your fists.

8. Meet the Audience

Get to your presentation early enough to meet some of the audience members. Then you will have some friends in the audience. As a bonus, you may even get some material to use in your speech!

9. Slow Down and Breathe

If you lose your breath, you lose your voice. Just prior to speaking, you can do some deep breathing to help calm yourself: breathe in through your nose and fill up your abdomen, hold this breath for 10 seconds and exhale slowly, pushing the air out with your abdomen. Repeat. Take a breath before you speak your first words. While speaking, remember to slow down if you speak quickly when nervous, pause and take a breath! You can also practice deep breathing while driving or at bedtime.

10. Speak to Individuals

For most people, speaking one-to-one is not as scary as speaking to a group. So, consider the group as composed of individuals and speak to individuals conversationally, making and sustaining eye contact with an individual for a complete thought before moving to another individual. As a side benefit, if you are prone to Uhs and Ums, you should see a decrease when you focus on eye contact with individuals. You can practice eye contact when you practice your speech by drawing simple faces on sheets of paper and putting them up in the room as you rehearse. Stuffed animals can work too, although it looks a little silly if someone walks in.

Combine the outer game of physical preparation, practice and performance techniques with the inner game of mental preparation to manage your fear of public speaking and to become the powerful and confident speaker you were meant to be.

Authenticity: Being the Real You

Sometimes the scariest part of speaking is the fear of judgment. And that fear of judgment keeps some speakers from being real and genuine. The unspoken thought process goes like this . . . *the way I am, who I am, might not be good enough. If I reveal the true me and I get rejected, then I have been rejected to the core. So, maybe it's better to project a masked version of myself . . .*

The most engaging speakers aren't the posers, the pretenders or the perfect, plastic people. They aren't the Tony Robbins wannabes. Now, don't get me wrong. Studying great speakers and even trying on some of their techniques can help you grow as a speaker, but just don't cover up who you are, what your passions and values are and yes, even what your vulnerabilities are.

The most engaging speakers have excellent speaking skills and great content, but beyond that they are refreshingly real. Their speech may be practiced, but their pain and pleasures are genuine. And they are not afraid to tap into the audience's experiences and transport them into the parallel universe of the speaker's own world. That's how a speaker and an audience bond.

People bond on a common ground of similarity. People bond when others are willing to open up. And by being a little vulnerable, by trusting that your audience won't judge you too harshly, you will gain the trust of your audience.

It's hard being vulnerable. Kids are vulnerable. But as we get older we put on the bullet proof vest of invulnerability. We cinch it tighter for fear that if we open up just a little, we might get shot down. Arrows might pierce our hearts.

But it is when you can be a little vulnerable with people that you can build trust and connect.

Shortly after Christmas last year, I had coffee with a new acquaintance, a man I had met at a Toastmaster meeting who also shared an interest in business storytelling. As we sat at across the table from each other at Starbucks, we shared a little about ourselves. He shared how he had been out of work for a while and I could see the guarded expression on his face, the invisible wall between us. I knew he wondered if I would judge him--If I would think poorly of him for being out of work.

I decided to be a little vulnerable.

I shared with him that I knew how he felt, because just two years earlier, my husband and I had been dealing with a failed business. Just two years earlier, not only had I gotten food at a food shelf, I'd gotten my kids Christmas gifts there too. But, it was temporary. Hard, but temporary—as it would be for him, too. Tough times never last, tough people do.

The wall came down. His face relaxed. He leaned in. We connected.

Taking off the bullet proof vest might be hard. It might be scary. It might just change your relationships. It most certainly will change your speeches.

That story was a little difficult to share with one person, but I still remember the first time I shared it at a speaking engagement. You could have heard a pin drop. All of a sudden I went from the shiny expert on the stage to the real person, transformed by the heat and pressures of life, who spoke from the heart.

A few cautions on developing authenticity:

1. If your emotions are too close to the surface, you may have to allow some passage of time to work through your emotions before you can share a particular story. Your audience is not your therapist.

2. Don't "overshare." Expose only what is appropriate and necessary to your point.

3. Talk to people in a conversational tone—don't go over the top and be too dramatic (although most people will tend to be too timid in telling a story). Be bold without being overly-dramatic. Imagine you are telling the story to your best friends.

Being authentic doesn't mean being perfect. It means being real. Take off the mask. Be the real you. Nobody else can.

Never Forget a Speech (or Almost Never)

One of the biggest reasons that people fear public speaking is that they are afraid of opening their mouths and "blanking out" or sounding stupid.

Some people even try to memorize their speeches.

Right off, you should know that I'm not a big fan of speeches that are memorized word-for-word. I've tried it and found that it increases my "blank out" experiences (because I have only practiced saying something one way, instead of a more extemporaneous flow of speech). When I memorize something it's like I set up a well-worn path in my mind. The problem with this is that under stressful conditions, I can get lost and if I only have traveled one path (practiced my speech the same way over and over), I can become mentally paralyzed, not having other options. By practicing more loosely, from keywords and concepts, I have traveled other paths, paths that become available under stress.

However, there are some instances in which you do want to memorize a speech or portion of a speech word-for-word (memorized historical speeches, for example).

Even if you don't need or want to memorize a speech word-for-word, you can use memorization techniques to enhance your recall of material.

The Steps to Never Forgetting Your Speech:

1. **Write the outline**—focusing on not more than 3 main points, if possible, and use a parallel structure, in which

each of your points starts with the same grammatical construction.

2. **Write (type or longhand) the body, then the introduction followed by the conclusion.** Does it flow? Especially work on transitions.

3. **Read your written speech out loud.** Does it sound OK? Record, if possible. I use the recorder on my phone. Pay close attention to transitions. A simple and very effective technique is to repeat a word that is at the end of one sentence in the beginning of another sentence as you transition to another part of your speech. I call it the **Echo Technique.** "She didn't take down the Christmas tree until Valentine's Day. Valentine's Day is 51 days after Christmas. I was ready to call the Fire Marshall."

4. **Use keywords.** If you don't need to have it memorized word-for-word, reduce your speech to keywords and work from the key words. An alternative to key words is to storyboard your speech (use pictures for points).

5. **Apply memorization techniques.** There are several you could use. Two are detailed below.

Memorization Technique #1: CHUNK IT! Read, Recall, Check, Repeat

Chunk the speech into smaller pieces (2-3 sentences)

- Read the chunk out loud
- Recall--try to say the chunk without peeking at the written speech
- Check by reading again (or if you recorded, you can listen to the recording)
- Repeat until you get the first chunk down

Then go on to the next chunk of material, but include the first chunk in the "Recall" step: Chunk 1 + Chunk 2, then Chunk 1 + Chunk 2 + Chunk 3 and so on.

Continue until you can say the entire speech, word for word. Use this only if it is absolutely necessary to memorize something word-for-word.

Memorization Technique #2: Silly Walk Method

Break the speech up into the main points.

- Assign each of the points to a room in your home—the sub-points can be pieces of furniture.
- Create a word picture for the point. In your mind see yourself doing something silly with the word picture in the room.
- Physically walk through the house if you can, picturing the silly pictures as you say the words for each point. You can also take pictures with your phone of the locations and then run through it visually on your phone, imagining you are taking a walk.

Practice each segment, in order, several times, until you have the wording down (you can apply the Read, Recall, Check Repeat method here also).

Another version of the "Silly Walk" is to create a map of your speech and use pictures to represent concepts (or destinations) for your points.

I've even created speech outlines that were only pictures (or simple symbols) and use the pictures as cues to what I want to say.

Review Techniques: Speed Speech (saying the speech very fast) and spaced reviews (review on a regular basis).

Use these techniques to reduce the "blank-out" experience. But if it does happen . . .

What to Do When You Blank Out During a Speech

Two-hundred pairs of eyeballs were on me. I had just delivered a dramatic, beautifully wordsmithed phrase in my contest speech. Then my mind went blank. I looked at the audience with the "deer-in-the-headlights" stare for what seemed like an eternity as my mind frantically groped for the next phrase.

Has that ever happened to you? Or, maybe you are afraid it will?

The dreaded blank out. It can happen if you haven't prepared adequately, but it can also happen even if you have been diligent in your preparation. Having a recovery plan can greatly reduce your anxiety, and you may be able to recover without your audience even realizing you had a memory lapse. After all, they don't know what you are going to say next, so if you change it up a bit, they probably will think you planned it that way.

"Blank Out" Recovery Techniques

1. Pause. Pause for a couple of beats, maintaining eye contact with a single person. The pause may give you the time to remember. Looking at one person (versus scanning) can be calming.

2. Rewind. Repeat the last sentence or phrase. This gives your mind both time to think and a little "restart" jolt.

3. Fast Forward. Jump ahead to content that you do remember. At some point in your speech you may remember what you were going to say earlier. You can work it in and may even prefer the new arrangement.

4. Take a sip of water. You will look in control and not rushed. Of course, your mind will be racing . . .

5. Check your notes. Hopefully you have just a few key words in a large font, so that your panic won't intensify as you scan your notes.

6. Go to the next slide. If you are using PowerPoint, you can use it as a teleprompter (although I don't generally recommend this practice!).

7. Smile. Smile like you have a secret and just look at the audience for a while. You will look very confident and the audience will be anticipating your next phrase almost as much as you are.

8. Have back-up content. Have a short, relevant anecdote or a back-up activity (a good idea anyway, to allow for flexible timing). Then, if you still can't remember, you can ask something like, "Now, where was I?" at the end of the story or activity.

9. Get the audience involved. Go for a short Q&A session. Or, have them pair up to discuss an important point or to do an activity.

10. Make fun of your memory lapse and build rapport. "I have completely blanked out." (laugh). Has that ever happened to you? . . . My grandson says I have 'old-timers' disease. Now where was I?"

11. Have a recovery plan. Proactively practice a recovery plan for your particular type of presentation (notes, no notes, PowerPoint).

Sample "Blank Out" Recovery Plan for a speech with notes:

- Step 1. Stop Talking
- Step 2. Pause/Get sip of water
- Step 3. Scan notes for next thought
- Step 4. Decide on what you will say next
- Step 5. Look up and make eye contact
- Step 6. Start talking

I wish I had proactively thought about what to do when my mind went blank before that contest speech a few years back. I managed to stammer on, but I never regained my flow after that stumble. On the positive side, I learned from that experience and you are the beneficiary!

How to Be a More Confident Speaker in 10 Seconds

You know your message. You know your audience. You've practiced. Now, it's show-time! How can you bolster your self-confidence in the few seconds before you speak— even as you are walking up to deliver your opening lines?

I believe that your confidence level can be affected by changing how you act, how you feel and what you believe—in any order! The usual order is to work on your belief and then that will change how you feel which in turn will change how you act. You can reverse that order right before you speak. In the few seconds before you speak, you need to focus on action!

Here are 5 steps you can take in the 10 seconds before you open your mouth to speak. Steps 1-3 can be done while walking up to speak, or in combination with steps 4 and 5:

1. Breathe. Take a deep, calming breath. Remember your brain needs oxygen!

2. Stand tall. Good posture not only helps with your breath support while you speak, it also makes you look more confident. I use a "string theory" to quickly improve my posture right before I speak. I imagine a string being pulled from the ceiling that connects the top of my head to my chest to my pelvis. Try it right now! It even works when you are sitting.

3. Mentally rehearse your opening sentence or two. Your opening should be ready to charge out of the gate with power.

4. Eye Contact. Look at your audience for a second or two, with the attitude of "this is a gift I'm giving to you" and a pleasant expression. Connect with their eyes. A confident speaker looks into the eyes of his or her audience.

5. Smile. As you continue for a couple more seconds with eye contact and before you actually speak, turn your pleasant expression into a broad, warm smile, the genuine kind that crinkles your eyes. Of course, if your speech has a very serious start, you don't want to smile inappropriately, but a smile is a magnet to your audience.

And then, deliver your opening lines with confidence!

Be an Audience Magnet with One Simple Act

Do you want to be a people-magnet when you speak?

Did you know there is one thing that you can do that will increase your trust-level, likeability, perceived confidence (and competence) and your attractiveness? (And calm yourself at the same time)?

That one thing is to smile—your genuine smile!

Smiling can reduce the levels of stress hormones and increase the levels of mood-enhancing hormones—in both you and your audience. Smiling relaxes your audience and the contagious nature of a smile encourages them to smile back at you! Plus, because a smile is the most easily recognizable facial expression—it can be seen from twice the distance of other expressions—smiling helps you connect with a large audience, too.

Knowing the importance of smiling means two main things for a speaker:

1. Smile often, especially at the start of your presentation.

2. Have the best smile you can.

First, smile often. Before you say a word, you can smile at your audience (look at them with love, excited to give them the gift of your presentation). During your speech, not every part of your speech will be appropriate for smiling, but odds are you can smile more. One thing I've noticed as I get older is that my neutral expression looks more negative than neutral, but a smile lights up my face with positiveness.

Smile during the happy or exciting parts of your speech. Smile after you have given your audience a "take-away" point or an action step. Smile and nod at your audience to get them to "buy-into" a concept.

Smiling is easier if it comes naturally, so make some effort in your day-to-day activities and smile at the checkout girl at the grocery store, smile at the waiter who serves your lunch, smile at the Starbucks barista and even smile at the grouchy woman behind the counter at the post office. Spend some time with small children—little smile machines!

Second, make sure you have the best smile that you can! Regular flossing and brushing and good dental work make a difference. Consider orthodontia if your teeth detract from your smile. Over-the-counter teeth whiteners can be an easy way to boost the brilliance of your smile. If you are a woman, frame those pearly whites in an attractive shade of lipstick.

Smile to draw your audience to you and your message like a magnet!

When you're smiling, the whole world smiles with you . . .

The Eyes Have It

Smiling isn't the most important thing you can do to engage an audience. Eye contact is the number one way to increase your engagement with an audience. A few additional benefits include:

- **Increased credibility** (people who don't make eye contact seem nervous and possibly dishonest).
- **Reduction in crutch words** (um, uh, er). I've noticed that people are more likely to use crutch words when they look up or off to the side as they gather their thoughts. Ever notice that people don't say "Um" or "Uh" as much in conversation?
- **You will sound more conversational** and, if you tend to talk too fast, you probably will slow down a little.

- **Your presentation will be more powerful**
- **Feedback from the audience—** people tell you a lot with their eyes! You can adjust your presentation more easily if you make eye contact.

Here's the MAIN THING to remember: Talk to one person at a time.

Think of every presentation as a conversation. You make eye contact when you talk with individuals, don't you? Your audience, whether it is 10 or 100 is made up of individuals.

If you just scan the audience (or worse yet, look just above their heads), you not only don't gain the benefits of eye contact, but you also risk looking like an oscillating fan! Sure, you can try to look at everyone, but you probably won't connect with anyone if the group is large.

Here are 3 tips that you can use right away:

1. Look into the eyes of one person for a complete thought (usually a sentence)

before you move on to another
person. Connect with a few people sitting
next to each other and then, work your way
around the room, connecting with a couple of
people to your left, middle, right, front and
back. Don't try to do this in any particular
pattern; just don't ignore an entire section of
the audience.

 Baby step: Consciously try it for at least
the first 3-4 sentences of your speech, and at
the end. You can expand on the skill on
future speeches.

**2. Practice with a "fake
audience."** Take a few sheets of paper and
draw crude faces on them (actually all you
need is the eyes). Tape them up on the walls,
at seated eye level. Then, practice your
speech, looking into the "eyes" of your
audience.

3. Talk to People NOT to Paper. Drill
this phrase into your brain. Look at your
notes to snatch up your next phrase or two,
but DON'T talk while looking at your
notes. People will barely notice your use of
notes if you only speak while looking at them.
Look up and then talk. Double space your
notes. Put then in a larger font (at least 14),

or better, yet, reduce your notes to key word notes.

How to Use Notes

Which category do you fall under, when it comes to using notes for a speech:

1. The Forgetter. You are afraid you are going to forget what you want to say, so you use notes.

2. The Writer. You worked hard to get your wording just so and want to say it just like you wrote it.

3. The "Wing-it" Speaker. Plan out what I'm going to say? You're kidding, right?

4. The Memorizer. You memorize your speech, almost word-for-word.

5. The "Talking Points" Speaker. You jot down a few key words to jog your memory.

6. The PowerPoint Slide Reader. Please— don't be THAT speaker.

I admit it; I have been in each of those categories. What I have learned, is that each of the categories has some benefits and in my best presentations, I combine many of them, at least in preparation for a talk. However, the approach that I have found to be most successful for me and many others is to use a "Talking Points" approach.

"Talking Points" preparation:

Step 1: Write out your speech. Pay careful attention to the introduction, the conclusion and the transitions. Here's a nifty trick to help trigger your memory as you transition to different parts of your speech: use the same word or phrase from the end of one sentence to the beginning of another as you transition. For example: "There are only 3 things we have to fear: 1. Bad men, 2. Bad decisions and 3. Bad breath. Bad breath is a bigger problem than you might think . . ." The phrase "bad breath" triggers my memory for the next sentence.

Step 2: Practice it a few times, revising it as necessary.

Step 3: Write out key words and phrases. You can also draw pictures/symbols. Try not to have more than 4-5 words per sentence or per line. Use a big font if typing. Double space. It might look something like this:

> Beginning, women, crucial, survival
>
> Men, hunters, women, gatherers
>
> Today, women, primary, sex-linked
>
> Mother, daughter, license, Target

Step 4: Set your written speech aside and practice from keywords (You can look back at first, but then resist the urge). Practice your introduction and conclusion so that you can do those from memory—those are the parts people will remember the most.

You don't have to say your speech the same way twice—No one will know if you use different words!

In fact, by allowing yourself the freedom to deviate from what you've written, you are less likely to "blank out" if your mind can't think of that one exact phrase.

Giving the speech:

The MAIN THING to remember is: **Speak to People, Not to Paper!** Don't look at your notes and have your mouth moving at the same time. Eye contact while speaking is important for audience engagement. Look down. Grab a few key words on a line. Look up. Speak. Repeat.

Never Speak Too Long

I'm not sure which is worse, a speaker who is oblivious to the fact that he or she has gone overtime or one who realizes it and keeps talking anyway, often trying to cram 15 minutes of material into 3 minutes. All I know is that I don't want to be one of those speakers. Neither do you, right?

Here are a few tips to help you stay within your time:

1. The Technical Approach. Figure out your WPM (Words Per Minute). Pick something conversational to read that's about half a page long. Ideally, it would be your speech! Count the words (or cut and paste it into a MS Word Document and get an automatic word count).

Time yourself reading the selection in a conversational manner (the stopwatch feature of a phone works well). Then divide the number of words by the time in seconds. Multiply by 60. That's your WPM. Do this a couple more times, with different selections and average the WPM. That's your ballpark WPM. Then, to figure out approximately how many words long you need your speech to be, you just multiply your WPM by the length of the speech (in minutes).

For example, let's say I read an article that has 576 words and I time myself reading for 4 minutes (240 seconds). I can calculate my WPM:

(576 words/240 seconds) X 60 seconds/min = 144 WPM (the average rate for an American speaker is 150 WPM).

Let's say I want to give a 10 minute speech.

My estimated word count is 144 WPM X 10 min = 1440 words. So, if I write a speech of approximately 1440 words, then it will be about 10 minutes long. However, it may be longer or shorter depending on pauses, rate variations, and use of humor.

Better to err on the side of being a *little* short.

2. Write a Flexible Speech. Sometimes you get more or less time than you were told. And sometimes your presentation goes faster or slower than you planned. This can happen quite easily if you have audience interaction or remember interesting stories to tell. Also, I have found that many people tend to speak more quickly when a speech is "for real" than when they practice.

One time I went to a conference and the speaker ended a 50-minute presentation 20 minutes early! She told me later that she had timed it at 50 minutes when she practiced. She had not been prepared with relevant "filler" material. Have a plan for adding or removing material on the fly, to meet time requirements.

In the real-world of presentations, you may be asked to speak for 45 minutes, but because the speaker before you may go too long, or the time may need to be expanded or reduced, the most important thing to know is what time you need to end. Be prepared to cut or add material or activities.

You can add or subtract examples, stories and sometimes activities or a Q&A session. Whatever you add or subtract, still end with your strong conclusion (which should come after a Q&A session).

3. PRACTICE. Time your speech while practicing. Obvious, right? But a lot of people don't do it! Do remember that if you say something funny, you need to allow time for people to laugh. Don't "step on the laughs" just because you are long on content and short on time.

4. Time your speech while presenting. Use your own timing device, if possible. But, be discreet about looking at the time. I use an app on my phone and iPad (Big Clock HD) that simply tells the time in a large format that I can see at a distance. Other apps will count down and show green-yellow-red indicators as you approach your time limit.

Speech Structure

A well-crafted speech can draw your audience in and take them on a journey to the destination that you choose.

A well-crafted, well-structured speech can also help you recall your points!

How to Write a Speech in 5 Minutes

You show up at an event and the organizer asks you to "say a few words" later in the program.

You arrive at your Toastmaster meeting and a speaker didn't show up, so the Toastmaster asks if you would like to take the "opportunity" to speak.

You show up at your surprise birthday party and realize people might expect you to say something.

How do you feel when asked to speak on short notice?

Probably not too excited. Probably a little (or a lot) afraid. Turn your fear into purposeful energy and use this opportunity to make a difference!

Here's a 5-Step process to prepare a speech in 5 minutes:

Step 1: THINK about your PURPOSE

(1 Minute)

- Why you? Why would you be the person to talk about this? If you haven't been given a topic, try using the following topic prompts:
  - **Event-related**—if there is a general theme
  - **Recent events**—news items or even something that just happened earlier in the meeting
  - **Lessons learned** from the past—pick a person, like your grandmother, to illustrate "lessons learned."
  - **One of your passions** or values in life—as it would relate to the audience.
  - **An analogy.** At a surprise birthday party, I started out "I feel a little like George Bailey in the movie *It's a Wonderful Life . . .*"
- Why this audience? Why would the audience want to hear what you have to say?

- What outcome? What do you want your audience to think, feel or do after you are done?

Write down your main message in one sentence. Everything you say must relate to your main message.

Step 2: BRAINSTORM (1 minute) Do you have one story that can provide the overarching framework? That's my favorite approach to short-notice speeches. Start your speech with the exciting "conflict" part of the story, but leave the audience hanging. Then, in the body, make story-related, audience-relevant points. Finally, use the ending of the story as your conclusion. You have given your audience a nicely wrapped, memorable package.

The story framework may not work in all situations, so consider other frameworks, such as:

- Problem-cause-solution
- First-second-third . . .
- Then . . . now . . . tomorrow.
- Location 1 . . . Location 2 . . . Location 3

Step 3: KEY POINTS (1 min). Come up with 1- 3 points and key supports. If you have a very short "say a few words" speech of fewer than 1-2 minutes, you can just make one point. For a longer speech, use three points. People can easily remember three points. Each point should have at least one support: a story, an example, a quote, or a relevant statistic. Write your points and supports in bullet format in the middle of your page, leaving room for the introduction and conclusion.

Step 4: INTRODUCTION (1 min). Jot down an idea for an attention-getting opening: a question, a story, a startling statistic, a quote. If you have time to look up quotes by topic (http://www.brainyquote.com), you can sound quite impressive using a relevant quote at the beginning or end of your speech.

Step 5: CONCLUSION (1 min). Your conclusion is what people will usually remember most. You may even want to write it before your introduction. You will want to call back your key points and end with a call-to-action or an inspirational thought. Don't add any new points in your conclusion.

At the very least, mentally go through your introduction and conclusion several times so that you can deliver them with power. If you have time to practice, like in the car on the way to a meeting, do so out loud to build fluency and confidence.

So, the next time someone asks you to speak on short notice, be daring and dazzle them!

Grab Your Audience! 3 Ps of Speech Openings

Do you want to hook your audience right at the start of your speech? Do you want to have them leaning forward with interest? Do you want to have an approach to introductions that you can apply to many speeches?

Now you will learn a time-tested pattern for speech introductions that will grab your audience's attention and create in them a desire to hear more.

There are three easy steps, **3 Ps**, of effective speech introductions: a little **P**ep, a big **P**romise and a clear **P**ath.   Get their attention (pep), tell them how they will benefit (promise) and preview how you will get them there (path).

Pep: Grab your audience's attention by opening with questions, startling statements, a quote, a poem, a story or a joke (although be careful with jokes—only use one if you know it will work). Your first few seconds set the stage with your audience. They will give you perhaps a 30-second honeymoon period, to give you a chance to grab their hearts and minds. See later sections on how to start and end your speeches.

Promise: Tell your audience how they will benefit by listening. Remember, everyone is tuned into their own radio station, WIIFM (What's In It For Me?). How will what you are about to say make their lives better?

Path: Give your audience a preview of where you are going to take them. This primes your audience and also gives your speech some organization! They can "take away 4 tools," "learn 3 steps," "gain 3 benefits," etc. I wouldn't have more than 5 "take-aways" in most speeches. Three is ideal.

As an example, take a look at the beginning of this section.

Pep: Do you want to hook your audience right at the start of your speech? Do you want to have them leaning forward with interest? Do you want to have an approach to introductions that you can apply to many speeches?

(Actually, the "Pep" is also an implied "Promise," but I do have a promise statement, too).

Promise: Now you will learn a time-tested pattern for speech introductions that will grab your audience's attention and create in them a desire to hear more.

Path: There are 3 easy steps, 3 Ps, of effective speech introductions: a little **P**ep, a big **P**romise and a clear **P**ath.   Get their attention (pep), tell them how they will benefit (promise) and preview how you will get them there (path).

Try the **3 P** approach in your next speech introduction!

The SHARP Method of Structuring a Speech

A speech is written for the ear and not the eye. Unlike reading an essay, a person cannot go back to review what you just said. Your audience is forced to go at your pace. Therefore, a speech must be clearly and simply organized to help your audience follow your line of thought.

Introduction (10-20% of your speech):
The introduction needs to accomplish three basic things, the 3 Ps mentioned earlier:
Pep—get attention (questions, startling statements, quote, story/humor)
Promise—state solution or benefit (give your audience a reason to listen. Sell a vision)
Path—preview points (tell them where you are going)

Transition

Body (70-85% of your speech):
The body typically will have three main points (people remember 3 points easily), with each point being supported by a both a mental anchor and a power phrase. Mental anchors help the point stick in the mind and are designated by the acronym SHARP (based on an acronym provided by Joe Sharp):

Story (or analogy/metaphor)
Humor
Activity
Reference/quote
Photo/prop

Power Phrases are catchy phrases that sum up the point in a memorable, repeatable way.
For example "Facts tell, but stories sell."

Transition between each point and transition to the close

Conclusion (5-10% of your speech)

The conclusion also needs to accomplish three basic things:
Revisit the points and promise from the introduction
Close with a big anchor—see following sections on openings and closings. Your most powerful anchor should go here, or find its completion here.
Call to action (the action might be a call to a different way of thinking, via a final thought-provoking question, or a call to feel differently about something and change an attitude, or it can be a call to a physical action).

You should not present any new information in the conclusion.

Notes on Transitions

Transitions help your speech flow smoothly as one unified, coherent presentation. They link from one part of your speech to the next.

A transition can be as simple as an extended pause. That's right. Silence. Just be silent for a couple of beats and then go to your next point. You can accompany "movement" to your next point with physical movement on the platform to another position. Many speakers will start out in the center in the introduction and move off to the sides for the main points and then come back to the center for the conclusion.

A transition also can be a simple "signpost" such as "first . . . second . . . third." Better signposting will include a number and a reminder phrase. So, instead of just saying, "Second . . ." it is better to say, "The second reason you want to use storytelling in speeches is . . ."

You also can use transitional words and phrases, such as "in addition to . . ." or, "Not only . . . but also . . ." and "in summary."

More elegant transitions show the connection between the introduction and the body, between the main points and between the body and the conclusion.

There are two main ways to show connection in transitions: the mini-summary (or recap), which quickly sums up the point before moving to the next point, or the mini-preview which sets up the next point.

You can recap your point or points yourself, or ask the audience a question and get them to recap the point for you. You also can share a story or quote which summarizes your previous point or previews the next point.

I will sometimes highlight an important point in the recap: "If you take only one idea from my presentation today, make it this . . . "

2001 World Champion of Public Speaking, Darren LaCroix in his winning speech used the mini-preview quite effectively:

- Set up point 1 (a story): Dr. Goddard had a ridiculous idea.
- Point 1: Dr. Goddard story
- Transition phrase: I remember when I had a ridiculous idea.
- Point 2: My ridiculous idea story

The transition to the conclusion is important and different in that you have to indicate to the audience that you are coming to a close (so that it doesn't seem abrupt). You can be obvious and say things like, "in conclusion" or "in closing" which is better than nothing or you could try a more elegant approach combining specific phrases (e.g. "Now that you can see how [solution] can work for you, let's review why you would want to implement it . . .), with body movement (coming back to the center) and slowing your rate of speech, using more pauses.

Here's a question on conclusions I've often heard . . . "Should I say 'thank you?'" I suppose it is a matter of personal preference, and if you are in Toastmasters, you probably have heard that you shouldn't. As for me, when I speak professionally, I almost always do. I sincerely appreciate my audience for allowing me to enter their world.

7 More Ways to Organize Your Speech

The standard 3-point speech structure may not be the best choice for every speaking situation. Here are other basic ways to organize a speech:

1. Chronological: What happened, first, second, third (story format) or a process
2. Past, Present Future: History, present situation, future
3. Cause and effect
4. Problem and solution
5. Spatial/geographical
6. Topical—divide main topic into sub topics
7. Acronym—typically used for topical organization or processes. For example, the acronym LEAP can represent the process of conflict resolution between two people: Listen reflectively, Empathize, Agree and Partner.

A typical business presentation might look like this, an expanded version of the problem/solution organization:

- Define objective (purpose)
- Describe current state (pain)
- Describe desired state (pleasure)
- Describe obstacles (preclusions)
- List possible solutions with pros and cons of each (pros and cons)

- Identify best solution, focusing on benefits (proposal)
- Close with action and/or agreement (path)

How to Start and End Your Speeches

Do you know what parts of a presentation are best remembered?

The interesting parts, right? Well, yes! And some parts are remembered better because of their locations in the speech. Numerous studies have shown (with lists of items) that people recall the items near the end of the list best (the recency effect). Items near the beginning are remembered second best (the primacy effect).

When it comes to presentations, there is also the first impression. How well you grab the audience at the start can dictate how engaged they are for the rest of the presentation.

The next several sections will cover the following topics:

1. Opening and closing with **questions**

2. Opening and closing with startling **statements**

3. Opening and closing with a **quote or poem**

4. Opening and closing with a **story**

5. Opening and closing with a **joke or humor**

6. **Bookending** (tying your ending to your beginning)

7. **Complete Conclusions**

8. Closing with a **call to action**

Open your speech to grab your audience's attention and tease them so they will want to hear more. End your speech powerfully to get your message remembered.

Engage Your Audience with Questions

Why start and sometimes end your speech with questions?

Questions engage your audience by causing them to think.   Questions can tap into prior knowledge. Questions can challenge assumptions. Questions can be used as a bridge to the next segment of your presentation. Questions take your audience from passive listeners to engaged participants.

There are 2 top mistakes that speakers make when asking questions:

1. Generalized question. If you want to make your audience members feel as if you are speaking to them individually, use the specific "you" and "your" and not the general "anyone" or "anybody" when you ask questions. Use you-focused questions.

Say, *"Do you want to make more money?"* and not, *"Does anyone here want to make more money?"*

2. No reflective pause. If you ask your audience a rhetorical question, and don't pause long enough for them to answer mentally, you have lost the opportunity to engage their thought process. Ask the question and stop talking long enough to mentally answer it yourself, before you go on.

Let's look at two basic types of questions: **rhetorical and response.**

Rhetorical Questions.

A rhetorical question is a thought-provoking question for which you do not actually want a verbal response. A rhetorical question can arouse curiosity and motivate people to try to answer the question, causing them to pay close attention to what you say next. So, if I start a speech with *"What does it mean to be human?"* I am using the question as a set-up. I might even follow it with a series of rhetorical questions, *"Does it mean . . .? Does it mean . . .? Does it mean . . .?"* that I then answer in the course of the speech. I might even end with a rhetorical question, *"So, are you merely going to be a human being or are you going to be human?"*

You can also use rhetorical questions as story openers to set the stage. *"Have you ever stood up to give a speech in front of 200 people, looked at the audience and had your mind go completely blank? . . . That's what happened to me . . ."*

Look again at the above example. Hidden in the structure is a powerful way of using rhetorical questions. Ask a "you" rhetorical question to get them to think about how they would feel and then move them into your world with a story, *"That's what happened to me . . ."*

Response Questions. Here are a few types of questions that require a response:

1. **Raised hands.** You can handle this by stating, *"Raise your hand if you . . ."* Or, *"By a show of hands* . . . (and then raise your hand up high to encourage hand raising). You can also just ask the question, *"Have you ever . . . ?"* and gesture to the audience with an open hand before you raise your hand. The open hand appeal invites them to answer and the raised hand models what you want them to do. It helps to nod at the audience while you ask the question.

2. **Audience members answer.** Let's say you want to have an audience member or two actually answer the question. This can be risky, especially near the beginning and I don't suggest it as an opening move if you haven't already established rapport. Even if you have a good audience connection, make sure it is an easy question and extend your open hand toward the audience as you ask it.

What if nobody answers the question? Definitely be prepared for that possibility. You could seed the audience ahead of time with one or two people who will answer. You could make eye-contact with someone, raise your eyebrows and extend your hand directly at the person and ask him or her specifically to answer (only do this if the person's body language indicates high engagement). You could say something funny like, *"I'm not going to grade your answer!"* which will loosen people up.

3. **Audience echo.** This takes guts and practice, but can be extremely memorable when used throughout the speech and at the end. Let's say you have a short foundational phrase or even a single word for your speech that you want people to remember. You can repeat the phrase or word several times as an answer to a question and then have the audience respond with the phrase or word when you ask the question.

For example, if I were giving a speech on sales attitude and I wanted to get the idea across that you can't dwell on rejection; I might have a foundational word, "Next!" I would probably tell three short stories illustrating three common sales situations in which I use the phrase "Next!" At the end of each story, I would have the audience practice saying "Next!" in response to a question related to that story. At the end, I would wrap up with the same three questions, one right after another, gesturing to the audience as a cue to say "Next!" And then make a concluding call to action using the foundational word/phrase.

What do you say when you can't get past the gatekeeper? . . . (audience) **Next!**

What do you say when someone says "No"? . . . (audience) **Next!**

What do you say when you want to quit? . . . (audience) **Next!**

Don't dwell on the past, but look to the future and say . . . **Next!** *(audience response).*

For your next presentation, engage your audience with questions!

Wake Up Your Audience with Startling Statements

Bambi vs. Jaws. No contest on which is deadlier, right? It's . . . Bambi. A deer is 20 times more likely to kill you than a shark. Every year in the United States, deer-car collisions kill more than 200 people.

The above startling statement, especially if accompanied by a visual, could open a presentation on the very practical topic of how to avoid hitting a deer. Or, it could be the opening of a speech about how we worry about things that are unlikely to happen (like getting killed by a shark while swimming in the ocean).

Opening your speech with a startling statement can jolt your audience to attention. Once you have their attention, it's much easier to keep it! Startling statements are less commonly used at the end of speeches.

The most common way to open a speech with a startling statement is to use statistics. You can find statistics on almost anything online! However, make sure your statistic is relevant to your topic and accurate. Here's one reliable source: http://www.fedstats.gov. Using that source, I came up with the following startling statement opening:

"As of 2011, the number of people with undiagnosed diabetes was 7 million. That's almost as many people as in the states of Minnesota and Iowa put together."

(As an aside, play with the wording. I had originally written these sentences as *"As of 2011, there were 7 million people with undiagnosed diabetes. That's almost as many people as in the states of Minnesota and Iowa put together."* Not as powerful—for 2 reasons: 1. the "shocker" was placed in the middle of the first sentence. It is much more memorable and dramatic to have at the end of the sentence. 2. The second sentence refers to the number 7 million of the first sentence. The second sentence has a more logical, more quickly understood flow with the number in closer proximity.

If you are going to use big numbers, try to give them additional context and to personalize them. By comparing the number to states, it becomes more than just a big number. Also, if you were speaking in a different area of the country, you could pick your comparison to be a relevant geographical area.

Startling statements don't have to involve statistics. They can just be unexpected. You possibly can take advantage of a disconnect between how you look/act and what you say.

Imagine a well-dressed business woman saying, *"I like to hit people. Actually, I like to kick them, too. I'm a second-degree black belt in Tae Kwon Do."*

Or, the same well-dressed woman saying, *"See this jacket? Three dollars."* I've used that line in a speech about overcoming adversity, in which I am wearing a very nice looking jacket, purchased at a Salvation Army Store during tough times.

What statistics or personal revelations can you use at the start of your presentations to wake up your audience?

Use Quotes or Poems to Open or Close Your Speech

The audience gazed in anticipation as I stood before them holding a large black cloth draped over my arm. I threw the black cloth over my head. After a brief pause, I quoted the opening lines of an Emily Dickinson poem:

"I'm nobody. Who are you?
Are you nobody, too?"

I then paused again, removed the cloth and continued with the rest of my speech. The speech was about noticing the people around us. It was for a Toastmaster speech contest several years ago. I didn't win (I think shrouding my head and might have been too contrived). However, quoting the poem, one of Emily Dickinson most famous poems, was a hit!

If you use a poem or quote to open or close your speech, you can inspire, motivate or challenge people with someone else's words. If the quote or poem is famous (and not too long!), you can tap into the audience's memories and associations and transport them to the message of your speech in a powerfully moving way. The words may carry an emotional charge beyond their meaning. For me the Emily Dickinson poem, "I'm Nobody" transports me to back to when I was a nobody in junior high school, and frankly, rather liked being a nobody.

The internet makes it easy to find quotes and poems! Here are just a couple of sources:

Search for quotes by topic at http://www.brainyquote.com

Search for poems by topic at http://www.poemhunter.com/poem-topics

Tips for using a poem or quote:

1. **Short**. Generally use short excerpts from longer works.
2. **Relevant.** It must be relevant to your message.
3. **Attributed.** Give credit. If the author is unknown, you can say, "Someone once said . . ." Don't say the author is "Anon" (Anon= anonymous. This is probably obvious to almost everyone, but I was at a high school speech contest and two of the contestants said their quote was by "Anon")
4. **Pause**. Pause before and pause after the quote, to give people time to absorb it.
5. **Practice!** You are using someone else's words which may trip up your tongue if you don't practice.

A fine quotation is a diamond on the finger of a witty person, but a pebble in the hands of a fool. ~Author Unknown

Open and Close Your Speech with a Story

Stories are my personal favorite way to open a speech. Stories touch our emotions and linger in our minds. Stories are a powerful way to captivate and connect.

Stories captivate us because we think in stories. We can't help it!

"Stories fill our lives in the way that water fills the lives of fish."
--Steve Denning

Stories connect because stories touch our emotions. Tell stories that elicit one or more of the seven basic emotions: happiness, sadness, anger, fear, disgust, contempt or surprise.

Stories also connect because they are concrete. We create visual images in our own brains when someone tells us a story.

And, perhaps most importantly, people remember stories! In the book, *Made to Stick: Why Some Ideas Survive and Others Die*, the authors tell a story about a class that one of them teaches. Bottom line: Stories get remembered about 13 times better than statistics. Facts tell, but stories sell!

Also, when you place a story at the beginning or end of your speech, you are taking advantage of the primacy and recency effect of memory. We remember best what we hear at the beginning and ending of information.

Nine tips for storytelling

1. **Use a storytelling format that leaves your listeners leaning forward.** A story usually only is interesting if there is CONFLICT. Here is a standard story format:

(Main character) is in (Circumstance/setting) and needs to (Goal), but faces (obstacles/opponents) when (Climax/conflict at a high point) until (resolution—obstacle or opponents are overcome).

2. **Don't always make yourself the hero in a story.** People will think you are arrogant. Some of the most effective and endearing stories are when the teller discloses some personal flaw (but don't get uncomfortably personal). You also can reveal your own character (which is a quick way to

build trust and intimacy) in your stories in which you learn a lesson from someone else or are a supporting character.

3. Ditch the back-story. Provide just enough background to make the story relevant or understandable. Get to the conflict as quickly as possible.

4. Don't provide all of the details. Let your listeners fill in some of the details with their own imaginations. As the 1999 World Champion of Public Speaking, Craig Valentine, says, "People buy-in to what they create."

5. Limit narration. Use just enough narration to set up dialogue. Dialogue is the heart of an engaging oral story. Make your characters come alive through dialogue.

7. Be dramatic—the number one drama tool in storytelling: the dramatic pause. Pause a couple of seconds before a climatic situation to heighten the feeling of anticipation. "To be or not to be?" (pause, pause) "That is the question."

8. Use primarily your own, personal stories! They are uniquely yours, even if you are relating a common experience. Especially good ones can be your signature stories. However, I am partial to using stories from popular movies to set the stage or provide an ending to a speech. But be careful in using stories from other sources (if you do, give credit). They can be overdone. Please, please don't tell The Starfish Story.

9. Act it out! Let your facial expressions convey emotions. Get your body into the story. Don't just say "we pushed the car out of the ditch," but actually act out at least the hand gesture of pushing.

To improve your storytelling ability, think "don't tell, show." People will remember what they see more than what you say.

Tell a story!

More on digging up stories in later sections.

Open and Close Your Speech with a Joke

Wouldn't you love to get your audience laughing at the start of your speech or leave them laughing at the end?

Jokes can do the job, but use them with caution! If you are using someone else's

material, you need to give credit. The joke
needs to be relevant to your presentation (I
hate it when presenters just tell a joke for a
laugh, but it has nothing to do with their
topic or the audience). Don't tell offensive
jokes.

Top tips on practicing and telling jokes:

1. Use funny material. Did you laugh
when you heard it? Did other people laugh?

2. Remember it. Record it.

If you just heard a joke and want to
remember it, try writing it down right
away. Or, you can tell it into your phone's
voice recorder, which also gives you your first
shot at telling it!

Save it in a joke file on your computer. Or, if
you have a blog, use it in your blog, but make
sure it is relevant to your topic.

3. Rehearse it.

I suggest starting out with short jokes—a
short set up and then a punch line. For
longer jokes, visualize all the characters as
you practice the joke. Use body language as
appropriate (moving your body will help you

remember). Practice the pacing. Don't rush it. Pause a little before and after the punch line.

Set up . . . (pause) . . . punch line . . . (pause)

If people laugh after the punch line, pause long enough to allow them to laugh. Don't step on the laughs. Milk the laughs with your reaction—just don't say anything. Let your body and face do the talking!

If people don't laugh after you have paused for a couple of seconds, you have a couple of options:

Option A: If it was very obviously a joke, you can make a self-deprecating comment such as, "Well, my cat thought it was funny."

Option B: Just move on. Don't react at all.

4. Practice in front of others. Practice on friends and family. They will love you even if you bomb. Nothing takes the place of practicing in front of others. Record yourself if possible. If someone laughs even a little, you can build on that. Maybe you can punch it up with attitude and body language or just change a single word.

"Words with a 'k' in it are funny. Alkaseltzer is funny. Chicken is funny. Pickle is funny. All with a 'k'. 'L's are not funny. 'M's are not funny. Cupcake is funny. Tomatoes is not funny. Lettuce is not funny. Cucumber's funny. Cab is funny. Cockroach is funny -- not if you get 'em, only if you say 'em."

—said by a character in Neil Simon's The Sunshine Boys

5. Sell it! Tell the joke with ATTITUDE. You must be very sure of the content, the order, the timing and most especially, the punch line. If in doubt, keep it out!

Try out some jokes—it does get easier with practice!

Bookend Your Speech (the Circular Close)

Bookends are designed "to buttress, or to support an upright row of books." Usually, bookends also are a matched, mirror image set, providing visual balance. Bookending your speech means that your speech introduction and conclusion support your speech in a way that provides balance. You "close the circle" for your audience, wrapping up your speech in a neat package.

Here are 5 ways you can bookend a speech:

1. **End by referencing your opening**. Refer back to what you started with (movie, words, quote).
2. **Contrast concepts.** Like mirror-image bookends, your concluding words can contrast with your opening words.
3. **Ask a question/answer a question.** Open with a question. Answer the question at the end.
4. **Use the same visual.** Use the same PowerPoint slide or the same prop.

Example:

Opening: I held up a photograph of an actor portraying Frankenstein's Creature and said, *"Frankenstein's Creature is a well-known image in popular culture—a grotesque monster—staggering and grunting like a simpleton. However, that is a gross misrepresentation of creature as originally created."*

Closing: I held up the same photograph and said, *"Frankenstein's creature was no simpleton. I leave you with the question-- Who really is the monster in this story? The creature, its creator or society?"*

5. **Story.** This is my favorite bookending method. Start your speech with a story, but cut it off at the climax. Close with the finish to the story. This approach also keeps your audience's attention. People want to know how the story ends! Just remember that the story has to be relevant to your speech content. You can even weave the story throughout your speech.

Longer example (for a speech about dealing with difficult people—this example includes more narration in the beginning than I would use in an actual speech. I would replace the narration with acting out the scene):

Opening: *I handed the old woman the Arby's bag. She peered into it. "But I asked for a Big Roast Beef Sandwich!"*

"It IS the Big Roast Beef Sandwich."

The old woman scowled and held up the sandwich for inspection. "But I wanted the really big one. This is puny!"

"Oh. . . .The choices were Big, Bigger and Biggest. I just got what you asked for. You said you wanted a Big Roast Beef Sandwich."

"But, that's not what I MEANT!"

I was frustrated. The old woman was cranky. She was demanding. She was . . . my mother.

Middle: I continue the story when I talk about having empathy with "difficult people." I reveal that my mother was struggling with a terminal illness. I make the point about "listening from your heart."

Ending: I finish the story about my mom by relating our last conversation, the day before she died, reinforcing the theme of "listening from your heart." The speech ends with a variation on a quote from the book The Little Prince and an inspirational call to action:

As I walked out the door, I heard her voice, almost inaudible:

"Di?"

"Yes, Mom."

"I love you, Di."

That was what was unfinished. The words of love. Those were the last words she said to me. She died the next day.

My mother listened with her heart and heard what I didn't say. What I didn't even know I needed to hear. They were the words in my heart that she heard with her heart. They were a gift. She was a gift.

In the book, The Little Prince, one of the characters says that

It is only with the heart that one can see rightly; what is essential is invisible to the eye.

I might change that to be:

It is only with the heart that one can hear rightly; what is essential is inaudible to the ear.

Listen from your heart and as you face conflict this year, and you will, try to look for the growth opportunity. Every conflict, every difficult person, comes with a gift. Listen from your heart.

Give your audience the gift of bookending your speech!

It's a Wrap! Conclude Your Speech

"Umm . . . I'm out of time. So, I guess that's all. Thank you."

We've all heard conclusions like that. Maybe you've even done it yourself. I call it the "aborted conclusion." Maybe that phrase, "aborted conclusion," makes you feel uncomfortable because of the usual connotations of the word, "aborted." Good. If you terminate your speech without a proper, complete conclusion, you have taken the life out of what might have been a unique, memorable experience for your audience.

Remember what you say last is most likely to be remembered best, so it is worth spending some time on your conclusion. In fact, I suggest writing out your conclusion before you write the introduction. Your conclusion should be the foundation that your speech rests upon.

A complete conclusion has three parts:

1.   **A transition**—Signal that you are

closing.
You can use very obvious signals (which are better than nothing), such as:
In conclusion . . .
To sum up . . .
In closing . . .
Another way to transition is to simply pause, letting your final point sink in. It doesn't work in written communication very well, but it can be quite effective in a speech.

2.   A summary—Summarize your main points. Repetition is important for recall.

3.   A memorable closing statement—a call-to-action (for persuasive presentations), a quote, a very short story, bookending (tying back to the beginning) or encouragement/inspiration—related to the key message of your speech. This is also a great time to use a call-back (referring back to a humorous bit).

Here's an **example of a conclusion** from a speech that I gave at a Toastmasters demo meeting:

Last point: *Tone of voice is important in communication, but body language is even more important.*

Transition: *Long pause*

Summary: *In order to be effective communicators, we not only have to pay attention to our words, but we also have to think about our voice and our body language, too! Effective communication combines the three V's—Visual, Vocal and Verbal for maximum effect.*

Toastmasters is a great place to develop these skills!

Closing statement (which, in this case referenced an opening story): *You may not change the world with your words, but you can change YOUR world. Change your world with Toastmasters!*

If you offer a Q&A session, end the session with a second memorable closing statement. Don't just end by answering the last question. Your ending is too important to leave it hanging on a question. Leave time for a final statement to wrap things up.

What about saying "thank you" at the end of a speech? There are conflicting opinions on this, so I'll just give you my take. It depends on the situation. For a Toastmaster speech, the custom is to **not** say

"Thank you." You typically end a Toastmaster speech with, "Mr. (or Madam) Toastmaster." For almost all other business speeches, especially sales presentations, ending with "thank you" is usual and customary. You could insert your "thank you" just before your final words, too, as in "Thank you for your attention. I hope you will use these tools of success to build a more prosperous life!"

The tools of success to build a strong conclusion are: transition, summary and closing. Craft them with care and leave your audience with a message that lingers.

Close Your Speech with a Call-to-Action

When you give a speech, you want your audience to think, feel or do something differently than before, right? Even if your speech is primarily informative in nature, don't you want your audience to do something with the new information? Don't you want them to consider your ideas and apply them in some way?

In my opinion, almost every speech needs some sort of call-to-action. If I have somehow been changed by a speaker, I want to DO something about it. The speaker does me a great favor by telling me what to do!

But don't just commando in a call-to-action at the end of your speech. You may have captivated your audience with your speech, but if you drop a call-to-action in out of the blue, they will feel like they've been taken prisoner by a poser, someone who seemed to be authentic until the end. You need to build up to a call-to-action with both logic and emotion. An effective call to action is the crescendo of your speech.

As you build toward that call-to-action in your conclusion, not only should you summarize the "logic" or main points, but you also should help your audience relive the powerful emotions they felt during a story or example earlier in your speech by referring back to it (or completing a story). In many cases, giving your audience the exact next step to take is appropriate ("vote for me . . . buy this program . . . if you promise to never text while driving, stand with me").

The basic steps to adding an effective call-to-action to your conclusion are these:

1. Transition from last point.

2. Summarize main points.

3. Pull the heart-strings. Refer back to something in your speech that creates a strong emotion.

4. Call-to-Action

Craft your call-to-action statement with care. Consider using rhetorical devices (discussed in the next sections) to create a memorable statement.

SCREAM to Give Your Presentations Power!

Colorful language can capture an audience's attention and it can anchor your points in their minds. The following acronym, SCREAM, was modified (by adding "simile") from the book, *Speak Like Churchill, Stand Like Lincoln* (A book I highly recommend for any speaker!).

In this section I'll give a brief overview of SCREAM and then discuss each element in turn in the following sections.

S-Simile

C-Contrast

R-Rhyme

E-Echo

A-Alliteration

M-Metaphor

Simile—using "like" or "as" to compare.

He screamed like a little girl. He hid under the table, as quiet as a mouse.

Contrast—pairing of opposites

Churchill: There is only one answer to <u>defeat</u> and that is <u>victory</u>. (It's a bonus if you can also use alliteration. For example: From the depths of **t**ragedy, he rose to **t**riumph)

Some opposite pairs: Present—Past (or Future), Beginning—End, Dark—Light, Friend—Foe.

Rhyme—Benjamin Franklin: An apple a <u>day</u> keeps the doctor <u>away</u>.

Echo—Repetition of a word or Phrase

Churchill: <u>We shall fight</u> on the beaches, <u>we shall fight</u> on the landing grounds, <u>we shall fight</u> in the streets, <u>we shall fight</u> in the hills; <u>we shall</u> never surrender.

Alliteration—repetition of the beginning sounds of a word.

Martin Luther King, Jr.: I have a dream that my little children will one day live in a nation where they will be judged not by the <u>c</u>olor of their skin but by the <u>c</u>ontent of their <u>c</u>haracter.

Metaphor—directly says that something is something else.

- His beard was a lion's mane.
- Bullets of hate shot from his mouth.
- His bark is worse than his bite.

You can even combine rhetorical devices:

Shakespeare (Romeo speaking of Juliet):

O, she doth teach the torches to burn bright! (Metaphor—Juliet is so radiant)
Her beauty hangs upon the cheek of night, (Metaphor—dark night sets off bright beauty)

Like a rich jewel in an Ethiop's ear; (Simile—
another expression of above metaphor).

Similes in Your Presentation

Are Like . . .

He was as phony as a three dollar bill.

She grinned like a Cheshire cat.

Your mind works like a computer.

"Like" and "as" are the typical words of comparison in similes. Simile is the first rhetorical device in the acronym SCREAM (Simile, Contrast, Rhyme, Echo, Alliteration, and Metaphor). Use the techniques of SCREAM to capture your audience's attention with colorful language and anchor your points the minds of your audience members.

Both similes and metaphors compare two different things which have some similar properties. Similes typically use "like" or "as" to make the comparison. A metaphor, which will be a later subject, substitutes one thing for another: "you are the wind beneath my wings." A simile would state it as "you are like the wind beneath my wings."

The simile compares ideas explicitly side by side. It is a literal comparison. "A" is like "B." The metaphor superimposes the ideas. "A" is "B." It is a figurative comparison, usually of a concrete, tangible thing taking the place of an abstract or less tangible thing.

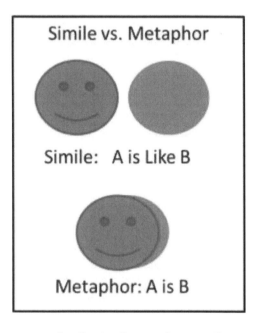

You can use both similes and metaphors to create vivid images in your listener's mind. But, similes can be more precise than metaphors and are often used to explain something unfamiliar in more familiar terms, enhancing understanding. *"Your heart is like a pump."*

How can you create your own similes?

1. Pick a concept, a quality, or an image.
2. Are there other words to describe the concept?
3. Consider possible synonyms (check an online thesaurus).
4. What else is like that (or for an ironic simile, the opposite)—brainstorm!
5. Add more interesting details.

Here's an example:

1. Something was all of a sudden easy to understand, even though it was complex
2. Another way to describe: It was all clear to me!
3. Possible Synonyms? Crystal, sunny, bright, smooth, cloudless, see-through
4. Clear as a crystal (or ironic: Clear as mud)
5. The concept, all at once, was as clear as a crystal. Its shining facets beamed new insights that forever changed my thinking.

Without similes or other rhetorical devices, your speech is like a vast desert of dullness. No more dry, boring speeches! A simile is like water for your presentation, giving life to your message.

Using Contrast in Presentations

What if in Shakespeare's play, Hamlet had said, "I wonder if I should kill myself?"

Nobody would have remembered it. Instead, Hamlet says, "To be, or not to be, that is the question."

Shakespeare knew the secret power of contrast.

Contrast is the second rhetorical device in the acronym SCREAM (Simile, Contrast, Rhyme, Echo, Alliteration, and Metaphor).

In short, contrast occurs when two opposite viewpoints are placed close together. It can be used for powerful phrasing, or even to structure an entire speech.

"Many are called, but few are chosen." -- Matthew 22:14

"Hot Eats, Cool Treats" —Dairy Queen

"Float like a butterfly, sting like a bee."—
Mohammad Ali

"The best means of insuring peace is to be
prepared for war."—Alexander Hamilton

If you need some ideas on opposite pairings,
check out http://thesaurus.com/

When you input a word, you get related
words, definitions, synonyms (similar
meaning) and antonyms (opposite meaning).

For example, in the listing for courage, under
the "boldness, braveness" definition, the
antonyms listed are:

"cowardice, faint-heartedness, fear,
meekness, timidity, weakness"

Choose a word (or investigate other
meanings) that fits with your concept and has
a catchy sound. In the case of *courage*, I'd
probably pick *cowardice* (which also has
alliteration) or *fear* (which is short and to-
the-point).

Not only can you have contrast in phrasing,
but you also can have contrast in your speech
structure.

In an insightful look at a few famous speeches, Nancy Duarte, author of *Slideology* and *Resonate,* gave a TEDx presentation, The Secret Structure of Great Talks, in which she reveals that the speeches she studied have a common structure, of talking about "what is" and then about the contrasting "what could be."

Take your speeches from dull to dynamic by using contrast!

Prime Your Audiences with Rhyme

Rhyme builds rhythm, momentum and memory.

Rhyme is the third rhetorical device in the acronym SCREAM (Simile, Contrast, Rhyme, Echo, Alliteration, and Metaphor).

Short rhymes can be very effective in foundational phrases in your presentations. Think of a foundational phrase as a "slogan" for a point you want people to remember. It can even summarize your main points. For example, I helped a presentation client boil down her 3 action steps to: Dump it! Claim it! Do it! In this case the rhyme is the same word, "it." Someone speaking about moving around to stay healthy could boil the message down to: Be fit. Don't sit.

Use ending rhymes with caution. If you have more than 2 sentences ending with rhyming words, it can start to sound like a nursery rhyme.

However, you can use suffixes that rhyme to create a sense of parallelism, which enhances memory.

A short example, I'm sure you've heard: Your <u>attitude</u> determines your <u>altitude.</u>

A longer example (Product Development):

Quality focuses on <u>specification.</u>

Research focuses on <u>exploration.</u>

Design focuses on <u>innovation.</u>

Production focuses on <u>creation.</u>

You can also use internal rhyme (i.e. not at the end of phrases), which is subtle, but powerful.

Winston Churchill: Out of intense <u>complexities</u>, intense <u>simplicities</u> emerge. <u>Humanity</u>, not <u>legality</u>, should be our guide.

So, how can you come up with your own powerful rhymes?

Online, of course!

1. **Try using synonyms** to explore words at Thesaurus.com . Maybe you want to use a different word than "angry" for example.
2. **Use a rhyming dictionary**, such as Rhymezone.com
3. **Search for words that end in specific suffixes** at OneLook.com (for example, if you want words that end in "ity" you can use a wild card asterisk in your search. You would search for *ity and then narrow your search by selecting "common words only"). OneLook.com is linked to the searches at rhymezone.com.

Isn't it time you added some rhyme? Prime your audience with rhyme.

Use the Echo Technique

You may have heard people say that giving a speech is simple: Tell them what you're going to tell them. Then tell them. Then tell them what you told them. That's one basic, boring use of repetition.

A more exciting use of repetition is the echo technique. Echo is the repetition of a word or phrase. It is the fourth rhetorical device in the acronym SCREAM (Simile, Contrast, Rhyme, Echo, Alliteration, and Metaphor).

An echo not only lingers in the mind, but also can build to a climax, gathering emotional force. If you are striving for a conversational speech, be sparing in your use of echo. Too much echo can seem over-dramatic and contrived. A little echo can go a long way.

The most common type of echo is **starting echo (anaphora)**, which occurs at the start of successive clauses.

My kind of party*: Good* food. *Good* friends. *Good* fun.

Note the set of three in the above simple example. Using a word or phrase three times has a natural, powerful cadence, but it is not an absolute rule as the next example illustrates:

"W*e shall fight* on the beaches, *we shall fight* on the landing grounds, *we shall fight* in the fields and in the streets, *we shall fight* in the hills; *we shall* never surrender."
(Winston Churchill)

A more recent example of starting echo:

Yes, we can, to opportunity and prosperity. *Yes, we can* heal this nation. *Yes, we can* repair this world. *Yes, we can.* (Barack Obama)

You can also use **ending echo (epiphora):**

When I was a child I talked like a child, I thought like a child, I reasoned like a child. (I Corinthians 13:11)

A difficult, but extremely memorable use of repetition is the **reverse echo.** When you reverse the echo, you are reversing the meaning as in these examples:

Ask not *what your country can do for you*, but rather *what you can do for your country.* (John F. Kennedy)

Eat to live, don't *live to eat.* (Ben Franklin)

Echo can also be used to evoke an **echo response** in your audience. One speech I heard that used this technique quite effectively was Toastmaster World Champion Speaker Ed Tate's "One of Those Days" speech. He told an ordinary story of how he was at the airport and everything seemed to be going wrong, ending each part of the story with "it was . . . one of those days." He ends the speech with "I knew it was going to be . . . (and the audience completes the sentence) "one of those days."

Don't let your presentations fade into the distant memory of your audience. Use echo to create rhythm. Use echo to create momentum. Use echo to create a powerful speech.

Polished Presenters Use Awesome Alliteration

Mickey Mouse, Donald Duck, Bugs Bunny, Fred Flintstone, SpongeBob Squarepants.

All cartoon characters.

All examples of alliteration.

Alliteration is the repetition of the same sound at the beginning of nearby words. It is the fifth rhetorical device in the acronym SCREAM (Simile, Contrast, Rhyme, Echo, Alliteration, and Metaphor).

Like rhyme, alliteration can be a powerful memory aid, anchoring points in the minds of your audience members. Alliteration is one reason we easily remember clichés such as *sink or swim, a dime a dozen*, and the favorite of every speaker, *perfect practice prevents poor performance.*

But alliteration can be very effective without being so obvious. I analyzed John F. Kennedy's 1961 Inaugural address and found several instances of subtle alliteration:

- **same solemn** oath
- **man holds** in his **mortal hands** (parallel alliteration)
- **for** which our **forebears fought**
- to **friend and foe** alike
- **whether** it **wishes** us **well** or ill
- we shall **pay** any **price, bear** any **burden**
- the **survival** and the **success** of liberty
- **colonial control**

- struggling to **break** the **bonds** of **mass misery**
- **sovereign states**
- **writ** may **run**
- before the **dark** powers of **destruction**
- the **steady spread** of the deadly atom
- **peace preserved**
- **bear** the **burden**
- a **grand** and **global** alliance
- high **standards** of **strength** and **sacrifice**
- let us go forth to **lead** the **land** we **love**

A couple of alliteration "Don'ts:"

1. Don't go overboard. Usually 3 words starting with the same consonant is enough. Extreme alliteration starts to sound like a childhood tongue twister such as "Peter Piper picked a peck of pickled peppers."

2. Don't use weird words. While you can get ideas for synonyms using a thesaurus, don't use words that you wouldn't normally say.

In other words, have fun, but not too much fun with alliteration. Don't say things like: "Abundant alliteration is always awesome" or even, "Polished presenters use awesome alliteration."

Master the Metaphor

"The greatest thing by far is to be a master of metaphor." –Aristotle

Metaphor is the last rhetorical device in the acronym SCREAM (Simile, Contrast, Rhyme, Echo, Alliteration, and Metaphor). Metaphor is the comparison of two UNLIKE things without using the word "like" as in a simile. With a metaphor you say that one thing is another thing, as in, "Jack is a pig." Of course, Jack is not literally a pig; he just acts like what many consider piggish—greedy, dirty or gross.

Metaphors usually link something that is tangible that we can physically sense (see, touch, hear, smell or taste) with an intangible concept. A metaphor can be a powerful shortcut to meaning, helping people see something in a new way. Metaphors and the other figures of speech in SCREAM will anchor your points in your listeners' minds. (Note the use of "anchor" as a metaphor).

Steps to Creating Your Own Metaphors

1. Decide on the mood you want to convey, but don't be too specific just yet. Pick a basic emotion:
Anger, fear, disgust, contempt, joy, sadness, surprise

2. Ask yourself, does this remind me of something from my childhood? Another experience? Is there some outstanding characteristic? Jot down whatever comes to mind.

3. Within the "mood" constraints, brainstorm by asking yourself 5-sense questions to make a concept more concrete. Go for quantity over quality at this point:
   a. What does it look like? (Visual impact is paramount in presentations. Go for greatest quantity here. You want VIVID images).
   b. What does it sound like?
   c. What does it feel like?
   d. What does it taste like?
   e. What does it smell like?

4. Draw it out. If finding a metaphor is difficult, try drawing pictures to loosen up your creativity.

The simplest way to construct a metaphor is:
The [thing 1] is [thing 2].

Examples:

His room is a disaster area.

Laughter is the music of the soul.

Scars are tattoos with better stories.

You can also use verbs to make less obvious metaphors.

A couple of examples:

His wife shot down every idea he had.

The fog crept in.

An extended metaphor can become an allegorical story, in which objects, persons and action are used to represent more abstract meaning. In the creation story in Genesis, Adam represents man, Eve represents woman, the apple represents temptation and the serpent represents evil.

In a speech about when my husband and I adopted our son as a 12 year-old from Russia, I wanted to convey the fear he had to face in overcoming life's obstacles, and used a dragon represent those challenges.

A flash of fire lights up the darkness. Through a smoky haze, two glowing golden orbs beckon to me. Like a moth drawn to a candle, I step closer. Suddenly, the smoke clears and the orbs narrow as the lizard-like eyes of a huge, green dragon glare at me with an unspoken challenge—a dare. The dragon looms over a young knight—a boy, weary beyond his years. Weary with battle. Weary with false bravado. Weary with a fight that one so young shouldn't have to face. Yet, there he stands, sword held high— proud, defiant even, his jaw set firm with determination. His eyes flicker with hope. Hope! How can he have hope? That he could survive, let alone succeed in slaying the beast seems impossible. The flicker of hope in his eyes fades and the scene darkens.

Later in the speech I talk about helping people slay their dragons and battling the monsters of the mind. And I refer to hope as a frail creature, but difficult to kill.

Allegorical stories can be difficult to work in to a speech, but stories based on your personal experience are easier to find and to relate to.

Digging up the Stories in Your Own Backyard

In the next several sections, you will learn different ways that you can "dig up" the stories in your life to be used as possible speech material. There's gold in your own backyard!

Digging Up Stories: Every Face Tells a Story

Almost any presentation, even business presentations, can be enhanced by using personal stories to anchor your points. But, how do you recall and apply those personal stories? One technique is to look at photos, specifically photos of yourself and try to recall where you were at in life and/or the story behind the photo. Often one photo can result in multiple story ideas. The four photos above and their brief explanations below will give you a flavor for the concept. That, and you will see some of the very fashionable glasses that I've worn over the years!

Every face tells a story!

Age 11 I am in 5th grade and am about 10 years older than my brother. We are about to have a formal picture taken, probably at Kmart. My mother took lots of pictures. I think it was to preserve the fantasy of a happy family. My parents were not happy together. I would go to my basement room and tune out their arguments by playing my violin.

Age 22 This picture was taken right before I left for my first day of work as an engineer for General Dynamics in San Diego. I look so young and innocent. I had no idea about the realities of being a woman in a male-dominated field. Or, of how ill-prepared I was by college.

Themes: Being Different, Discrimination, Experience vs. Head Knowledge

Age 27 I became a full-time mother and homemaker, while at the same time building an Amway business with my husband. We were going to be rich and have perfect children. I became an invisible woman—my husband's wife and my children's mother.

Themes: Managing Multiple Priorities, Identity Crisis, Unrealistic Dreams

Age 48 This is my first photo for my professional speaking business. I didn't have much money to spend because our technology business wasn't doing well. At the end of the year, we had declared bankruptcy. I smiled to hide the pain.

Themes: Starting a business on a Shoestring, Dealing with Loss, Rising from the Ashes

Need a story to anchor your point? Try looking at some pictures!

Digging Up Stories: Memories from Floor Plans

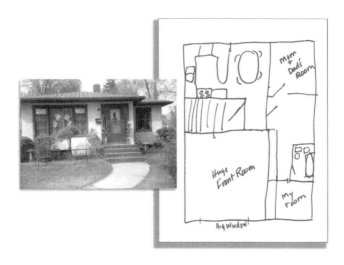

You can mentally dig for stories in your own back yard! (Or, at least from a drawing of your backyard). One exercise that can help with your recall of stories is to draw the floor plan of one of your childhood homes (or even a "map" of the back yard).

For example, when I drew the rough floor plan of my childhood home, it was like I stepped through a time portal as I mentally stepped through the front door. In my mind, I was walking through the house, a house I hadn't been in for 20 years. I could see the family pictures on the bumpy-textured walls. I could feel the stickiness of the plastic covering on the couch (yes, my mother put plastic on the couch and left the plastic covers on the lampshades, too). I could smell my mother's oregano-laden spaghetti sauce simmering on the stove. When I arrived at my bedroom, I opened the closet and saw the picture I had drawn of my grandmother when I was a teenager and I remembered how she stood up to Santa Claus when Santa forgot to give me a gift at a family Christmas party.

As I mentally walked from room to room, I was amazed at how arcane details would jump into my memory--like when I was a little girl and I would sit, transfixed at my mother's transformation as she applied her makeup. She was so beautiful that even my little second grade friends would remark on what a pretty mommy I had. But, I knew the truth. It was work. I can still remember her saying, "It hurts to be beautiful." She said the same thing when she would make me sleep in the pink sponge curlers to make my thick, stick-straight hair fall in perfect waves around my shoulders. At seven years old, I didn't care about being beautiful. But, I now could use that story to help make a point. What we see as beautiful, or accomplished might seem to have been effortless, but there often is effort or sacrifice involved. And, some people don't want to make the sacrifice.

What stories will you rediscover when you mentally walk through your childhood home floor plan?

Digging up Stories: Highs and Lows Graph

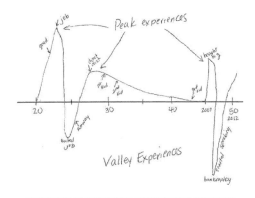

Another way to recall stories, is to draw a "Highs and Lows" graph, or as David Sibbet discusses in his book, *Visual Meetings*, Peak and Valley Experiences.

Decide on a time period (your whole life, a year) and draw a horizontal time
line across the middle of a blank sheet of

paper. Then mark off time segments and graph and label the high and low experiences of your life. Do you see a pattern? Do you notice that in life you are generally heading toward a high point, or a low point, sometimes with greater speed or greater severity?

Are stories coming to mind? As you were at a high or low point, or heading out of one, did you learn some lessons?

Digging Up Stories: Ask Questions

A great way to dig up stories that could be used as speech material is to ask yourself some questions. You also can ask other people these questions (great for interviewing older family members or retiring employees). Here are a few to get you started:

-What did you want to be when you were a kid?

-What did you enjoy doing the most as a child?

-If your childhood ambitions changed, when was that and why?

-What was your inspiration for starting your present career or business?

-Was there a specific "aha" moment?

-Did you face rejection? What were the obstacles? How did you overcome them?

-Who helped you along the way?

Ask interesting questions and get interesting answers!

Humor: Finding the Funny

Have you ever tried to think of something funny to say and drawn a blank?

Have you ever wanted to incorporate humor into a presentation, but didn't know how?

Of course you could search online to find some funny jokes or stories, but uncovering the humor in your own life will give your presentations a unique flavor.

My favorite way to incorporate humor is to tell a humorous story. A humorous story can be merely amusing to be effective, but you can also punch it up a bit by applying humorous techniques.

Try these three simple tools to get started:

1. Set-up/Punch

2. The Rule of Three

3. Self-deprecating humor.

Set-up, Punch

In Rodney Dangerfield's classic "Take my wife . . . please . . ." the humor exists because we expect something like "Take my wife . . . for example . . ."

In the set-up of a joke, you are setting up an expectation, taking your audience on a mental train ride and then the punch line derails them. It is the twist, that element of surprise that is the punch line's power. And there is the element of "timing."

One delivery technique to master that is common to all forms of comedy is "timing." You need a little pause before the punch line (or funny word) and a little pause afterwards.

If nobody laughs, you can just go on and if they do laugh, don't "step on the laugh" by continuing on too quickly. Allow people to laugh. Milk the laughter by reacting with your own facial expressions and body language. In short, "sell it!" Your delivery can make or break humor.

The timing looks like this:

Set up . . . (pause) . . . Punch line . . . (pause)

Brevity is best when doing a set-up/punch line joke. Try not to have more than one or two sentences to set up a joke.

Pay attention to what makes you laugh. As I was preparing this section, I received an email with this quote:

"Women who seek to be equal with men lack ambition."—Timothy Leary

If I were saying this line in a speech, I would time it like this:

"Women who seek to be equal with men . . . lack ambition. . ."

The Rule of Three in Comedy

There is a principle in comedy that things that come in threes are funnier than other numbers of things. The basic idea is that a series of three creates a progressive expectation, or tension, which is built up and finally released on the third thing.

Because two is the smallest number of things needed to establish a pattern (and our minds crave patterns), when the third thing is unexpected, and fundamentally different, our minds are derailed.

At it's simplest it is this: expected, expected . . . unexpected.

For example:

I've traveled the world: Paris, London . . . Fargo, North Dakota . . . Yah, you betcha. I'm a world traveler.
(note: the pattern I set up was large, well-known European cities that people would be impressed with. Fargo, of course, is not. Fargo is also a funny-sounding name for a city. Adding the "Yah, you betcha. I'm a world traveler" adds a little self-deprecating humor).

Play with the rule of three, but add sparingly to your presentations.

Self-Deprecating Humor

Put yourself down to bring the laughter up!

In addition to being funny, self-deprecating humor makes you seem:

- more confident—confident enough to point out your faults
- more modest—not a puffed up egomaniac
- more likeable—your failings can make you more relatable

A great resource for developing your own humor is Judy Carter's book, *Stand Up Comedy: The Book,* I've paraphrased and simplified some of the material in the book to give you a 3-step process for developing material that pokes fun at yourself. I call it the **LAF** process.
1. **L**ists—write lists of traits and issues
2. **A**ttitude—add attitude
3. **F**ormulas: Apply some humor formulas

1. Lists

Brainstorm under the following categories. I've bared my soul and listed some of my personal issues.

- **Negative Personality traits/shortcomings**
- **Unique traits (esp. physical)**
- **Things that make you angry**
- **Things you worry about**
- **Things that frighten you**

2. Attitude

- Rant and rave on a topic without trying to be funny. I hate . . .
- Then try to take a mocking attitude. I love . . . or I'm proud of . . .

3. Formulas (all involve incongruity)

- Exaggeration
- Set up . . . Punch line
- Rule of 3 (expected, expected . . . unexpected)
- Use a prop?

Here was my attempt on ranting and adding some humor formulas to my trait of being "directionally impaired" (more politically correct than "directionally disabled"):

I hate getting lost. I guess I'm directionally disabled. It's disability that gets no respect. There are no special classes in schools for students who can't find their way to the bathroom. People make fun of me—"she gets so lost . . . she can't find her way out of a paper bag."

I hate getting lost. Nobody wants me to be the driver. My children don't even like going places with me—they don't buy the "scenic route" line any more. The last time I told them we were going to the Mall, they ran to their rooms . . . and packed overnight bags.

I hate getting lost. Now that I have GPS Navigation on my phone, you wouldn't think it is such a problem. But I think my GPS is defective—or not very good at math. Almost every time I take a turn it says "recalculating."

I hate getting lost. When I get lost 3 things come to mind: where am I? Will I be late? And, I'm sure glad I always have . . . my overnight bag!

LAF your way to being funny!

How to Self-Evaluate Your Speech

Do you want to greatly improve your presentations?

I could just say, "hire me," but you can improve your presentations all on your own, too.

You can self-evaluate.

A good self-evaluation is a journey of awareness.

A great self-evaluation is one that starts with preparation and planning well before you give your speech.

To prepare you need to have the equipment to record. You can buy an inexpensive video recorder and a tripod or buy just a voice recorder. Most phones have a recording feature (video and/or audio). If you want to be unobtrusive in your recording, just do the audio.

Additionally, plan one or two specific goals for speaker improvement that you will work on during the speech. Record and evaluate yourself practicing. Record your live presentation and evaluate that, too.

Watch or listen to yourself at least once, but 3 times or 4 times will allow you to evaluate at a deeper level.

Speech Self-Evaluation Checklist

1st viewing/listening: The first time is partly to recover from the shock of hearing or seeing yourself!

__overall effect,

__audience response

__anything that particularly stands out, positive or negative.

__How did you do on the one or two specific goals you had set?

__Did your speech fit the audience and context of the event? (e.g. speeches to teenagers in a high school classroom would typically emphasize different things, and be delivered differently than speeches to senior citizens on a cruise ship)

2nd listening: The second time **just listen (turn off the visual)**, focusing on content, **making an outline as you listen:**

___Did you get the audience's attention at the start? And, was your "attention-getter" relevant to the topic?

___Did your introduction clearly give your audience both a reason to listen, and a clear direction (a clear thesis)?

___Could you outline your own speech (was the organization easy to follow)?

___Did you support your points with examples, stories, statistics, metaphors, analogies?

___Did the transitions maintain flow?

___Did you ramble?

___During the speech did you connect with head (logic), heart (emotion), hand (action) and leave your audience with something to think, feel or do?

___Did you end powerfully? Did you call back your key points? Did your ending provide a feeling of closure? Did you have a call to action?

3rd listening: The third time, again **just listen, focusing on voice (turn off the visual)**:

___Did you vary your vocal pace, pitch and volume in a way that enforced your message and kept it engaging?

___Do you need to project more?

___How was your use of language?
  ___ Appropriate to audience?
  ___No jargon or slang that the audience wouldn't relate to
  ___Good enunciation and correct pronunciation and grammar
  ___Little to no filler words (use of Ahs, Ums)
  ___Did you use rhetorical devices (e.g. simile, contrast, rhyme, echo, alliteration, metaphor, rule of 3)
  ___Did you pause long enough after important points or rhetorical questions or after you said something funny (did you let people have the time to laugh or did you "step-on" the laughs)?

4th viewing: The fourth time, if you have video, watch **the video again, leaving on the audio, but focusing on the visual:**

___How was your eye contact?

___Did you speak from memorable key words or did you look down at wordy notes too much?

___Did you use sustained eye contact for entire thoughts? Or, did you flit or scan?

___Did your facial expressions, body language (stance, movement) and gestures distract from or enforce the message?

___Did your gestures look natural?

___Was your attire appropriate? Video, especially, makes you reconsider busy prints!

___Did you move on purpose mostly (or was there noticeable pacing, rocking, hand-wringing, etc.)?

___If you used visual aids, were they easy to see and integrated smoothly?

A wrap up question:

If you had the opportunity to deliver this speech again next week, what are the top 1-3 changes that you would make?

Self-evaluation and recordings can also be shared with another speaking professional or a presentation coach.

Self-evaluate for more powerful presentations!

Encore! Tips and Helps
The next few sections are a collection of delivery tips, easy PowerPoint principles, Q&A management tips and a sample speaking engagement checklist.

Delivery Tips

1. Don't tell a story using notes. Ever (unless reading is part of the story—a letter, for example). **A story comes from the heart**. Practice telling the story without worrying about saying it exactly the same way every time. Be prepared to drop your script if

something happens just prior to your presentation that you can incorporate.

2. In a group setting, make sure you can be **seen and heard** by the audience (use a microphone, if necessary. Adjust lighting). If you are using props or PowerPoint, make sure that they are big enough for the audience to see.

3. In general, **speak conversationally**. But, do modulate your voice to make a story interesting. A blind person should be able to enjoy your story.

4. **Record** (voice) and video whenever possible. Self-analysis is very enlightening.

5. Powerful presentations include **pauses** and **sustained eye-contact**. Practice holding eye contact for a complete thought. Don't be an oscillating fan!

6. **Natural gestures** are best when not specifically using body language to describe something. If doing a "scene," practice staging from the **audience's perspective** (that means

"past" is on your right and "future" is on your left)

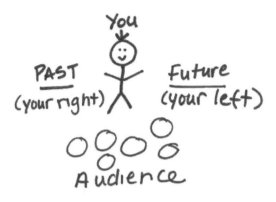

7. **Don't step on your set pieces**. When setting a scene, make sure that your imaginary locations and items don't float to different locations. If you are piling up bricks to your right, the bricks need to stay there and not float to your left. If you refer to a location later in your speech, you can simply point to the imaginary location to help your audience create the picture.

Easy PowerPoint Principles

All too often a PowerPoint presentation is the Kiss of Death for an audience. You don't want to be THAT presenter do you?

While you may not NEED PowerPoint (or other, similar presentation software), the truth is that in business, it is often expected, and if done well, can provide engaging visual support to your presentation.

There are 4 easy-to implement style techniques that you can start using with your very next presentation: Go Big, Create Contrast, the Rule of Thirds and Less is More.

And, this should go without saying, but speak to your audience, not your PowerPoint slides. If at all possible, position yourself so that you are on the audience's left (your right) of the PowerPoint screen (to reduce the visual "jumping" from you to the top left of the screen, which is where people's eyes naturally go).

1. Go BIG—Use Big Pictures

In the average slide, there is a title on top and a picture in the middle or off to the side. This is better than a bullet-point list, but there is something very simple you can do for greater impact: Go BIG! Let the picture take up the whole slide, with no borders. When a picture fills the entire slide, our minds imagine the picture bleeding off the edge and we mentally fill-in the rest of the picture.

Instead of having a lot of words and reading the slide, you can just talk about what is on the slide.

Before:

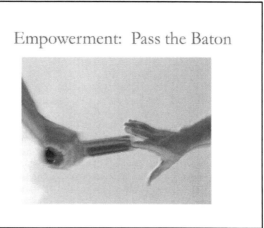

Empowerment: Pass the Baton

After:

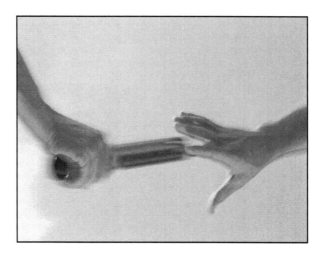

2. Try the Photographer's secret—**The "Rule of Thirds"**

Create visual interest by being a little "off." Instead of having centered subjects for all of your slides, try setting your subject about one-third from the edge (top to bottom or side to side). Imagine your slide divided into horizontal and vertical thirds--the intersection of the points are the "power points" of the slide

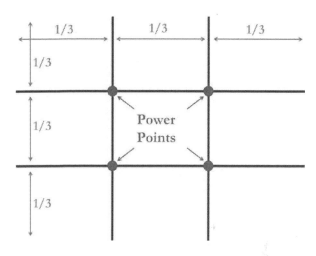

Before:

After:

Composition using "Rule of Thirds"

3. Create Contrast

The mind notices differences. Creating contrast can be as simple as making sure your text color and your background are not too similar.

Before (slide reads: *Is this easy to read?):*

After:

4. Less is More—the KISS Principle for PowerPoint Presentations.

With a picture you can convey more with less! Fewer words can actually help people understand meaning by cutting through complexity. People usually don't need more data. What they need is meaning and application of the data. So, don't confuse with the data—just give what is necessary for your audience to understand your point.

Create more compelling presentations today with these 4 principles: Go Big, the Rule of Thirds, Create Contrast, and Less is More.

Check out this Slideshare presentation to see this concept explained: http://slidesha.re/EasyPowerPoint

13 Tips for Handling the Q&A Session

Do you dread the question and answer (Q&A) session?

To calm your nerves and come across as a confident presenter, try these Q&A session tips at your next presentation:

1. Practice responses to questions that you think might be asked. Role play questions.

2. Plant a question or two in the audience before you start. You can have a great short answer prepared to the planted question and the planted question can "break-the-ice" for others to ask questions.

3. Let them know near the start! Let the audience know near the beginning of your presentation that there will be a Q&A session. That way, they may jot down questions to ask and won't be surprised when you give them the opportunity to ask questions.

4. Ask assumptively. Slightly change how you ask for questions. Instead of "Are there any question?" try asking, "What questions do you have?" Or, "Who has the first/next question?" Ask for questions in a way that lets the audience know that they should have questions.

5. Answer your own questions. If you didn't plant a question or no one asks a question, try saying something like, "Many people have asked me . . . [a typical question]?" and then answer your own question, followed by, "What questions do you have about [related topic to the question you just answered]."

6. Listen to the entire question without interrupting the questioner.

7. Ask for rephrasing not restating of questions you don't understand. If you don't understand the question, don't ask the questioner to restate the question (Why would you want them to repeat what you didn't understand?). Ask the questioner to rephrase the question. If you still don't understand, ask clarifying questions.

8. Repeat the question to the audience to make sure that you have understood it and that the audience members have all heard the question before you answer it.

9. Diffuse the loaded question. If you get a loaded questions, such as "Why are you charging so much for your program?" try using "empathize and redirect." Empathize with the person, "I can understand your concern about the price." Then redirect the question to one that you actually want to answer, "I believe your concern is whether you are getting a good value for the price . . ." If the person is unsatisfied or becomes hostile, offer to speak with them personally after the presentation.

10. Cut off the long
comment. Sometimes you get a person who makes a long comment instead of asking a question. This isn't always bad. But, if the person is eating up too much time, cut them off at the end of a sentence (they have to take a breath at some point) saying, "Thank you for that comment." Then look away from the person (so as not to encourage the person to keep speaking) and ask, "Next question?"

11. Keep your answers short. Don't
deliver another speech.

12. "One last question." Keep an eye on
the time and make an offer to take "one last question."

13. End with a strong concluding
statement. Don't end lamely by just answering the last question. End with the bang of a final story, an inspirational quote or a strong call to action.

Sample Checklist for a Speaking Engagement

— Confirm time/location/agenda/AV set up
— Presentation Notes
— Equipment (computer, cords, remote, flash drive, etc.)
— Clothing (jacket on hanger), back-up clothing
— Introduction (for person introducing you—large font, name phonetically spelled)
— Cell phone
— Contact phone numbers
— Map to location
— Handouts (bring some, even if the host is making copies)
— Props
— Water bottle
— Timing device (I use an app on my phone/iPad)
— List sign up (newsletter)/lead form
— Camera/batteries/tripod (if recording)
— Give away item(s)
— Business cards
— Promotional Materials
— Items to sell
— Cash for change, credit card processing
— Thank you follow-up to host

Final Challenge

Don't let your fear or lack of experience hold you back from finding your voice and changing your world. And, don't worry about being perfect. You won't be. But you can strive to be better while being true to yourself. But you must take action.

Learning techniques without applying them is like watching a show on how to catch fish, but never casting your own rod. You might know a lot, but it doesn't mean anything if you don't actually catch fish. If you do not currently have ample opportunity to practice giving presentations, I urge you to find a Toastmasters club near you. Toastmasters International (www.Toastmasters.org) is a worldwide organization dedicated to helping people hone their communication and leadership skills in a learn-by-doing, supportive environment.

Don't let the cat get YOUR tongue!

Toastmaster Testimonial:
Finding My Voice

Do you remember the first time you realized that the spoken word had power? Was it when you were small and asked someone to be your friend, and they said yes?
Or, maybe someone used words to hurt you and your mom said, "Sticks and stones will break your bones but words will never hurt you." You knew that wasn't true.

Or, maybe, like me, you found by accident. Words just came out of your mouth and people reacted.

This is me at three.

Big teeth.
Big smile.
Bad hair day.
Some things never change!

However, one thing that did change for me at three was that I began to realize the power of the spoken word.

My mother had brought me to work to meet her boss and coworkers. One look at her boss and I was in awe. She was just about the ugliest woman I had ever seen—long pointy

chin, hooked nose, dark, bushy eyebrows over beady eyes. I blurted out, "Mommy! She looks like the Wicked Witch of the West!" Suddenly, there was complete silence. Wow. I had made quite an impression!
My mother turned to me and said, "Diane, don't you mean, Glenda the Good Witch?"

Hello? Did my mother just lose her mind?
"No. Glenda was pretty!"

Fortunately, my mother's boss started laughing and all was well. And I had found a new power—the power of words.

But as I got older, the power weakened, dimmed by the lack of self-confidence that can occur during the teen years.

As I entered the work force as a woman engineer, I paid more attention to my abilities to calculate than to my abilities to converse.

Later, as a stay-at-home parent, I began to feel that I was becoming invisible and didn't have much to say. I was losing my voice.

I can thank Toastmasters for helping me find my voice.

When I visited a Toastmasters club in late 2003, I didn't know that Toastmasters would lead to a new career path. I didn't know that Toastmasters would lead me to some of my best friends. I didn't know that Toastmasters would not only make me a better speaker, but also a better leader.

I'd like to tell you that my joining Toastmasters was part of a bigger plan for my life—a powerful plan for powerful words—but it wasn't—well, maybe it was—it just wasn't my plan.

When I first visited a club, I wasn't looking to become a polished speaker or to enhance my leadership skills. I was just looking for a club that would allow my homeschooled, teenaged son to participate, even though he was too young to join. They welcomed his participation, on one condition—I had to join the club!

I joined the club and the next week, I was in a leadership position, as educational vice president, helping to plan club meetings. Over the past few years I have held several club and district leadership positions, greatly improving both my management and leadership skills—"on-the-job" leadership training in the non-threatening and supportive environment that is a hallmark of Toastmasters.

In addition to growing in leadership skills, I grew in communication skills through the various projects emphasizing different aspects of communication from the basics of organizing a speech to the challenges of leading discussions.

I was finding my voice again—rediscovering the power of words.

And I also found the best kind of friends—the encouraging kind!

It was with the encouragement of other Toastmasters that I began to consider developing myself as a professional speaker.

I found my voice.

Toastmasters can help you find yours.

Visit: www.Toastmasters.org

Made in the USA
San Bernardino, CA
20 December 2012